100 CAREERS

TO KNOW IN FILM AND TELEVISION

ASHLEY TAMAR

TABLE OF CONTENTS

3D or CG Animators..1

Animator also known as 2D Animator, 2D Puppet Animator, 3D Animator, Computer Graphics (CG) Animator, Stop-Frame Animator, Stop-Motion Animator......................................2

Art Director...3

Base Camp Generator Operator...4

Best Boy Grip...5

Bookings Coordinator...6

Boom Operator...7

Casting...8

CG Animators – see 3D Animators...9

Cinematographer..10

Clearance Coordinator...11

Colorist...12

Composer...13

Compositor...14

Computer Animator..15

Concept Artist...16

Construction Manager...17

Costume Designer..18

Covid/Health & Safety...19

Craft Service...20

Data Technician (Input/Output aka I/O)..21

Deliverables Producer..22

Digital Imaging Technology aka DIT...23

Dimmer Board Operator...24

Director...25

Director of Photography aka DP...26

Distribution Executive...27

Dolly Grip..28

Editor...29

Environment Artist...30

Film Archivist...31

Finance Controller..32

Gaffer...33

Graphic Designer..34

Greensperson aka Greensman, Greensperson, Nurseryman, Greenskeeper, Greens Foreman............35

Grip..36

Illustrator...37

Information Technology/Technologist (IT) 38

Intimacy Coordinator..39

Key Hairstylist..40

Key Grip 41

Key Makeup Artist 42

Lighting Artist (VFX) 43

Lighting Board Operator also known as the "Light Op" or "Board Op"...............................44

Lighting Technician 45

Line Producer..46

Location Engineer 47

Location Manager..48

Loggers..49

Matchmove Artists 50

Modelling Artist 51

Motions Graphics Designer 52

Music Contractor..53

Music Coordinator..54

Music Data Analyst 55

Music Editor...56

Music Supervisor...57

Office Production Assistant (PA) 58

Payroll...59

Photo/Picture Editor 60

Picture Car Coordinator..61

Postproduction Supervisor/Producer...62

Print Production Associate/Assistant 63

Production Accountant...64

Production Assistant (PA)..65

Production Buyer 66

Production Designer...67

Production Health & Safety Supervisor..68

Production Secretary..69

Property Master (Prop Master) 70

Publicist 71

Rigger 72

Rigging Grip 73

Roto Artist aka Junio Visual Effects (VFX) Artist 74

Runner...75

Screenwriter/Script Writer 76

Script Editor..77

Script Supervisor 78

Set Designer 79

Set Dresser 80

Set Medic and Construction Medic 81

Scientific Consultant 82

Showrunner...83

Software Developer 84

Software Engineer 85

Sound Mixer 86

Stakebed Driver...87

Steadicam Operator..88

Stop-Motion Animators 89

Story Editor...90

Stunt Coordinator..91

Subtitler 92

Supervising Sound Editor 93

Texture Artist aka Texture Painter, Texturing Artist, Visual Effects Artist (VFX), 3D Modelling &

Texture Artist..94

Transportation Captain and/or Transportation Coordinator 95

Virtual Production (VP) 96

Visual Effects (VFX) Supervisor...97

Vocal Contractor..98

Video Playback Operator aka Video Assist Operator (VAO) or Video Tape Operator (VTR) 99

Walkie PA..100

Writer's Assistant..101

Dear Creative,

Welcome to my 3rd edutainment book. As always, I curated this literature with you in mind.

In 2014, I started traveling and performing in the Broadway hit show "Motown the Musical." After conducting and teaching multiple Master Classes, I remember feeling empty. I continually asked myself, "If all of these talented students are pursuing the same thing — being onstage and the next star, then who's going to balance the system and pursue other unpopular, less considerable non-traditional careers in the Arts?"

Fast-forward to the pandemic. Because no one, and I mean, no one was authorized to occupy live venues and perform, I immediately knew it was time to put my Bachelor of Music Business degree from the University of Southern California to use. I began weekly Music Supervision sessions/training with my mentor Dawn Soler, former Senior Vice President of TV Music at ABC Signature, a The Walt Disney Company branch. After securing my first job, "That Damn Michael Che" show, I realized a constant and obvious lack of seeing more black and brown talents in key non-traditional careers in television and film. And that's where a lightbulb went off.

If you, like me, attend a movie and remain in your seat until the end of the credits roll then this is the book for you. In "100 Careers to Know in Film and Television," I desire to educate you on the unlimited and vast careers in television and film.

Now's your time to learn a new skill or new software, and test your knowledge about all that God has given you. Now's the time to explore more careers that your school may not teach. Now's the time to think big. Now's the time to grab a pen, and let's go in. With love,

1

3D or CG Animators

3D animators use computers to fill in the frames of their computer-drawn models. The movement of their models is pre-programmed through a moving skeleton, or rig. 3D animators animate the most important frames - key frames. This is known as blocking the shot. Then they either draw the in-between shots by hand or allow the computer to do the rest of the work through the rig in a process known as interpolation. During pre-production, 3D animators test the rig and check it will work for their characters.

Examples of Production(s): *Digby Dragon*

2

Animator also known as 2D Animator, 2D Puppet Animator, 3D Animator, Computer Graphics (CG) Animator, Stop-Frame Animator, Stop-Motion Animator

Animators' mimic biology as well as creative so they can bring character to life.

Animators create still images that are played in a rapid sequence to create the illusion of movement. They are artists, actors and storytellers. They know how characters show emotion and have a good, technical understanding of the way things move. They make a believable world through the blend of realism and artistry.

Animators take a visual brief from a storyboard and a verbal brief from a director. From the brief, they create the drawings, models or computer images in a way that gives the illusion of movement. This ability to translate the brief into movement is at the heart of all animation.

3

ART DIRECTOR

An Art Director in film is responsible for the visual and aesthetic aspects of a production, including how it communicates visually with the audience. They work with artists and pre-visualization crew members to establish the film's overall aesthetic before other work begins. Art directors use design elements like color, light, and effects to create moods, promote themes, and capture the audience's attention. They also make decisions about artistic style and when to use motion. Art directors also manage the art department and personnel, including set decorators, costume designers, and special effects technicians. They oversee set construction, scenic work, and quality control, and keep track of schedules and budgets. Art directors also collaborate with the production designer, director, and producers to translate the production designer's vision into reality.

Professional Art Director to Know - **Nick Fulcher** *(Cardi B, Yoko Ono, Kodak Black, Jon Bellion, and Radamiz)*

4

BASE CAMP GENERATOR OPERATOR

In this profession, you are responsible for powering the vehicles at the base camp. Base camp includes all the production vehicles except for the working trucks, electric shooting trucks, grip shooting trucks, camera trucks and prop trucks. The Base Camp Generator Operator oversees the installation and operation of all electrical equipment to power the various pieces of equipment that the transportation department provides. He or she works with a Base Camp Generator Operator to ensure proper routine maintenance is performed. The Base Camp Generator Operator also oversees the safe and proper operation of all electricity generators that supply power to all trucks and trailers. He or she must make sure that the generators are always fueled and troubleshoots any mechanical or electrical problems that may arise. The Base Camp Generator Operator works closely with the entire transportation department.

5

BEST BOY GRIP

The Best Boy electric is the second in command to the and acts as the foreman of the electrical team. They supervise the daily operations of the electrical crew; make sure all cables, generators, and other important pieces of equipment are on set, working properly, and in their right positions for each shot; assign duties to the team and manage their schedules; prepare and handle all paperwork (including expenditures within the department); order and return gear; oversee the loading and unloading of production trucks; and monitor repairs, oversee pre-lighting on a set, and communicate what's needed for each scene.

Professional Best Boy Grip to Know – **Miguel Sánchez**

"I make budgets [for] manpower and specialty equipment—lifts, cranes, anything needed to put lights in the air—or very special lights.... I'm entrusted with hiring and doing timecards, assigning people to different jobs."

~ Miguel Sánchez ("Parks and Recreation," "House of Cards," "Thor").

6

Bookings Coordinator

Bookings Coordinators are the great organizers of the post-production schedule. They know what equipment the facilities house (post-production company) has, and they know the post-production process. They allocate, organize, and monitor the flow of the technical and creative people involved.

They talk to the producers, help with quoting and costing jobs, and deal with the administration of each project. This involves preparing job sheets, invoices, and confirmation forms. They work out what the client needs and provide the creative or technical staff with whom the producer may want to work. They closely follow the progress of each job, checking the producer is happy with the finished product.

7

BOOM OPERATOR

A Boom Operator, also known as a First Assistant Sound, is a key member of a film production's audio crew who is responsible for capturing high-quality audio on set. They work with the production sound mixer and utility sound technician to position and operate boom microphones, select and place radio microphones, and maintain audio equipment. Boom operators use a large, long-range microphone mounted on a specialized arm or "boom" to capture dialogue and other sounds. They must maneuver the boom to capture clear audio while remaining out of the camera's frame to ensure a seamless visual experience for the audience. Boom operators also need to take note of planned camera movements and lighting requirements during rehearsals to avoid issues like microphones falling into shots or casting shadows during filming. If the boom can't capture a sound effect or line of dialogue, they may pull the actor aside between setups to record "wild sound" that can be used later.

8

CASTING

The casting department in film and/or television is responsible for finding actors to match the roles in the film. This usually involves a casting director or casting agency, who work with producers and directors to understand the script and the director's vision. The casting director's job is to select actors who have the right personalities, looks, and characteristics for each role. They also consider how well the actor will fit in with the other cast members and their chemistry with them

Professional Casting Director(s) to Know – **Robi Reed** *(Various Spike Lee and BET projects) and* **Kim Coleman** *("Dear White People" and "Lovecraft Country")*

9

CG ANIMATORS – SEE 3D ANIMATORS

10

CINEMATOGRAPHER

A Cinematographer is the second-most crucial creative voice on set, right after the director. A Cinematographer is responsible for the photographing and recording of a film, TV series, music video, or other filmed live action production. They create a visual narrative by deciding on how to capture all the onscreen elements—including camera angles, lighting, framing, color, and filters—as well as deciding the camera, film, and lens type. Cinematographer is often interchangeable with Director of Photography (DP) whereas both titles refer to the person on set who is responsible for crafting the visual style of a production. "Cinematographer" tends to be used for projects with more aesthetic elements. Cinematographers bring a director's vision to life by making artistic and technical decisions. They bring together all the onscreen visual elements to create a specific look and feel. They also determine how each shot should be blocked, composed, framed, and lit-map out all camera angles and movements and guide the camera operators, gaffers and key grips throughout the shoot. Some cinematographers operate the camera themselves.

From preproduction to postproduction, they work closely with the director, helping to craft the visual style and mood of the entire project. During preproduction, costume designers, hair stylists, makeup artists, and production designers all report to the cinematographer, workshopping ideas together before launching into their respective work. This collaboration sets the film's comprehensive look.

Skills Needed to be a Great Cinematographer
1. Proficiency in camera operation and techniques
2. Considerable experience and ability in shooting and lighting
3. Technical skills to craft mood using color, light, and shadow
4. Comprehensive understanding of aesthetics
5. A great eye for detail
6. Strong leadership
7. Communication
8. Interpersonal skills

Professional Cinematographer(s) to Know: **Kira Kelly** (*"13th," "Queen Sugar" and "Insecure"*) **Ernest Dickerson** (*Various Spike Lee projects*)

11

CLEARANCE COORDINATOR

Rights clearance is the process of obtaining permission to use works owned by third parties. Materials may be protected by trademark, copyright, privacy and other laws. The first step in the clearance process is determining what creative works have been or will be used in the production.

Professional Clearance Coordinator to Know - **Kelly Miller** *("The Game")*

12

COLORIST

A film Colorist works with the director and cinematographer to design a film's color scheme and grade and correct the colors in the footage. They also adjust other color-related errors in the footage. Colorists contribute to the film's mood and look by choosing colors that fit the tone and style of the drama, and that can evoke certain emotions in the audience.

Skills of a Film Colorist:

1. Color scheme
2. Collaborate with the director and cinematographer to select a color palette that fits the film's tone and mood. This could include deciding whether to use primary or milky colors, or whether the colors should be restrained or hyper-colored.
3. Color correction
4. Normalize any color inconsistencies or errors in the footage, such as those that might result from different cameras, lighting setups, or locations. This is important to do before color grading so that all the footage has a consistent starting point.
5. Color grading
6. Adjust the color, contrast, and brightness of the footage to enhance the visual aesthetics.
7. Use color-editing software like Base light, Davinci Resolve, or Adobe Premiere Pro to achieve the desired look. Keep up with software developments and learn the best tools for the job.

Film colorists should have a good understanding of color theory, including how different colors can affect people psychologically. They should also have knowledge of the digital and film processes and be able to get the creative look they want from raw files or negatives.

Degree(s) to Consider - Art and Physics

13

COMPOSER

A film Composer is a music professional who creates original scores for movies. Their work enhances the film's emotional impact and narrative by mirroring and supporting the action on screen. Composers often collaborate with other film project leaders, such as directors, producers, and screenwriters, to ensure the score matches the film's style, genre, and aesthetic. Film composers typically begin developing their score after a movie has been partially or fully filmed. One collaborative process between the composer and director is called a spotting session, where they watch the film together and discuss which scenes need music, the characters' emotional states, and the general mood. The composer, their assistant, or a music editor will take notes and write down timecodes for when cues should come in and out.

Skills of a Film Composer:

1. Knowledge of music history and construction
2. Ability to compose in different styles and genres
3. Improvisation skills
4. Ability to read scores
5. Quick theme creation.

Professional Composers to Know

- **Kurt Farquhar** (*"The Neighborhood," "The Game," "Black Lightning"*)
- **Ali Shaheed + Adrian Younge** (*"That Damn Michael Che Show"*)

14

COMPOSITOR

Compositors create the final image of a frame, shot or VFX sequence. They take all the different digital materials used (assets), such as computer-generated (CG) images, live action footage and matte paintings, and combine them to appear as one cohesive image and shot.

Compositors consider visual aspects of a scene. Realistic lighting is a key one of these. Anything caused by light hitting a lens is a compositor's responsibility. They relight to improve the look of the image.

Compositors do 'chroma keying' (also just called keying). This is where they select a specific part of an image that has a distinct color or lighting and extract it to be used elsewhere. This method is commonly used with 'green screen' or 'blue screen' footage, where a subject has been shot in front of a singularly green or blue background, to be able to place the subject in a different setting or environment later, in post-production.

Compositors work as the last part of a VFX 'pipeline' (the name given to the VFX production process). They can be employed by VFX studios or work as freelancers.

Professional Compositor to Know: **Simon Richardson** – "Confessions of a Junior Compositor"

15

COMPUTER ANIMATOR

A Computer Animator designs and creates animations for film, tv, videogames using computer software.

16

CONCEPT ARTIST

Concept Artists create artwork to inspire the look of the visual effects (VFX) in a film or TV production.

They draw the characters or creatures and environments as well as vehicles, props and buildings. They begin with a brief, which might be a script, or the original concept of a film as told by its filmmaker. They carry out research and create mood boards, which they use as a starting point to create lots of versions of their designs. The artwork that concept artists create helps other members of a production, or in the VFX pipeline, to have a shared vision.

Concept artists use digital and traditional drawing and painting to create their work. A lot of the work they produce is in the form of still 2D images; however, concept artists can also produce work using 3D software to create 3D wireframe computer-generated images (CG). This can help speed up the VFX production pipeline.

Concept artists typically work on a freelance basis, and their job role is highly specialized. They may grow to be associated with a particular VFX company.

On large-scale movie productions, concept artists can work in a film's art department or costume department. They act as the point of contact between the film departments and the VFX team.

Professional Concept Artist to Know: <u>Ralph McQuarrie, Star Wars Concept Artist</u>

17

Construction Manager

Construction Managers look after the building of studios and sets. They make sure that sets look as realistic or otherwise as desired. They interpret the drawings of the production designer, art directors and draughts persons and work out how to build them in ways that are safe and environmentally friendly. Then they hire the workforce, the carpenters, painters, riggers and plasterers, and ensure everyone knows what needs to be done and by when. They are responsible for getting the necessary materials and tools on site and for the safety of the crew working with machines and at heights.

Construction managers are responsible for dismantling the sets, known as 'striking' the set, and ensuring all the materials are recycled as far as possible, or put into storage, considering other environmental considerations.

Skills of a Good Construction Manager:

1.   Construction: Know all aspects of building work

2.   Reading Drawings: interpret drawings to plan size and scale, understand the designer's vision, work out what this means in terms of building requirements

3.   Organization: Manage a budget, work to a schedule, recruit hundreds of constructors within a tight timeframe

4.   Communication: Be able to liaise between the artists and the construction workers, get a team to work well together

5.   Staying Safe: Ensure all health and safety measures are in place.

18

Costume Designer

A Costume Designer designs, sources, and creates the clothing and accessories worn by the characters in a film, series, or theatrical production. Their main job is to telegraph who a character is via what they're wearing. To achieve this, costume designers—who head the wardrobe department and are responsible for staffing and managing the team—must tap into their inner psychologist, sociologist, researcher, historian, and actor. Juggling these roles helps them to design, create, compile, and fit the most appropriate outfits and accessories to each character to serve the needs of the narrative and the director's vision. A costume designer's day is a long, demanding one. During preproduction, they read the script, take notes, and analyze the plot, tone, and setting of the project. They also coordinate daily responsibilities, schedules, and deadlines for the production team, and are hands-on during fittings.

Professional Costume Designers to Know

- **Ruth E. Carter:** *("Black Panther," "Roots," "Amistad")*
- **Mylette Nora:** *("The Tonight Show" - Jay Leno)*

19

COVID/HEALTH & SAFETY

In this profession, you ensure a safe production environment. With meticulous adherence to health and safety guidelines, he/she oversees protocols, conducts regular screenings, and manage safety measures to safeguard the well-being of the cast and crew.

20

CRAFT SERVICE

Craft services is a department on a film set that provides food, drinks, and other assistance to the cast and crew. Craft services is also known as "crafty" in the United States and Canada. Craft services is important because it helps keep the cast and crew energized and hydrated, which can prevent them from performing poorly and maintain production quality. Craft services are always available, so actors and crew can grab snacks between takes and eat meals during breaks. Craft services may offer a variety of snacks, including healthy options, as well as teas, coffee, and other drinks. They may also provide basic medicine and special requests. Craft services is different from catering, which is usually handled by a catering company or restaurant and provides full meals.

Professional Culinary Artists to Know – **Chef Razia Sabour** (*Fuller Food*)

Data Wranglers *often referred to as **Digital Imaging Technician** (DIT's) and/or **Loaders***

Data Wranglers back up files on a location shoot. If they don't do this correctly, all the work that's been done to capture the action could be lost. On a shoot using digital cameras, data wranglers take the cards containing the raw files (known as 'rushes') from the cameras and sound recorders. They transfer and back up data on to memory drives. They check the data, label and log them, making sure there's no data loss or corruption. Data wrangling is usually done to at least two external hard drives. Next, they transfer the data to the post-production department of the unscripted TV production. They keep a log of who has received what footage and what copies of the data exist. Depending on the production, data wranglers may have to perform runner or logger duties too. More experienced data wranglers might also be involved in setting up the cameras and adjusting the live pictures in a shoot. In those instances, they might be called a **'digital imaging technician' (DIT).** Some data wranglers might also be expected to maintain the camera kit when out on location. Then they might be known as **'loaders'.**

21

DATA TECHNICIAN (INPUT/OUTPUT AKA I/O)

Data Input/Output (I/O) Technicians are responsible for organizing, transferring, and storing the computer files and data for a VFX production company. They manage the computer storage and retrieval systems, including company hard drives. VFX companies process large amounts of data because they deal with high-quality video files and digital 3D animation files. They know different digital camera formats, for instance, Alexa, Cannon, Phantom and Red. Data I/O technicians troubleshoot any issues that come up to do with file storage. Data I/O technicians ensure that all of transferring and storing of data is done securely and that files are encrypted wherever necessary. They follow company protocols to comply with safety standards. They make logs of all the files they receive and perform quality control checks on these files to see if there are problems or if the files are corrupted. They use file transfer programs to perform their role. Data I/O technicians give technical support to people working in a VFX pipeline when needed. They are usually employed by VFX companies or studios rather than freelancers.

Skills of a Data Technician

1. Programming and coding skills

2. Have knowledge of programming in C++ and Python with a high level of technical ability

3. Computing technical skill - be able to work in Microsoft Windows, macOS (Apple), Linux or Unix operating systems

4. Understand how the data sharing application FileMaker Pro works and be able to use it

5. Understand file transfer protocols (FTPs)

22

Deliverables Producer

When a film or TV drama is made, it must be made in a variety of different formats; DCP (for cinema), IMF (for streaming platforms) or conventional file or DVD mastering. Part of the work of production is to create these and QuickTime files for reviewing and sharing the film and further sales.

The deliverables producer oversees that process. They work with the film's postproduction supervisor to decide the schedule for producing the picture and sound deliverables and what additional material will be included in the delivery, such as bits of footage that weren't used for the final film. They work with their team to encode video and audio into file-based formats in the most effective way possible. They make sure that the assets are tested and delivered within the agreed budget and on time.

Skills of a Deliverables Producer

- Programming: Be able to program in several languages such as a few common ones to know and/or learn:
- Visual Basic
- VB NET
- Java
- Python,
- C
- C++
- JavaScript
- HTML
- Knowledge of file-based and DVD technologies: Stay up to date with the latest authoring tools
- Organization: Schedule, work to time and within budget
- Attention to Detail: Have an interest in minutiae and the ability to deal with repetitive tasks
- Problem-Solving: Take initiative and figure out solutions to problems as they arise
- Communication: Work with film and TV drama producers

23

Digital Imaging Technology aka DIT

In pre-production, in music videos, commercials, DIT is what cameras, what formats to record, what color spaces, what deliverables. They work with colorists and hand in hand with gaffers, monitoring signals to tv. They assist the cinematographer with color correction on set and troubleshoot aspects of filming on digital rather than film, including camera settings, color management, dailies management, and workflow.

24

DIMMER BOARD OPERATOR

The Dimmer Board Operator oversees operating the lighting console/switch board and creating lighting plots and equipment schedules for various sets, stages, or locations. He or She must also document the lighting set-ups for archival purposes.

In this profession, you are responsible for setting up the lighting console, which controls the lighting on set. Then, he or she must trigger every lighting cue for a performance or a scene. In case any final adjustments need to be made to the lighting effects, the Dimmer Board Operator should know how to program them.

In this profession, you are in complete control of the dimmer board. This means that he or she must constantly inspect, repair, and maintain the console and each piece of equipment associated with (fixtures, power and data cables, etc.) it to lessen the chances of malfunction.

25

DIRECTOR

Along with the producers, Directors are at the top of the crew hierarchy. They are creatively in charge and lead production from start to finish. A significant part of a director's job is doling out instructions to every department to ensure that each aspect of the finished product fits their blueprint.

Professional Director(s) to Know:

- **Sadé Clacken Joseph** – *"Rap Shit," "Trap Jazz," and "Diarra from Detroit" (BET)*
- **JJ Anderson** – *"Sacred Soil: The Piney Woods School Story" (HULU)*
- **Tim Story** – *"Fantastic Four" and "Barbershop"*

26

Director of Photography aka DP

Behind every distinctive shot is a director of photography (DP). The director of photography uses their artistic eye and technical know-how to create a film's visual elements. They are responsible for everything that involves capturing images with the camera, including the camera itself, shooting angles and camera movements, film and lens type, lighting, framing, color, and filters. Working with the director and production team, the director of photography conceptualizes and crafts the way a film will look. They develop the film's tone, color, lighting, special effects, and mood, at times through mood boards or look books.

During preproduction, traditionally, the DP participates in location scouting, breaking down the script to create a shot list and storyboard, determining what equipment is necessary, and hiring their team and heads of the departments they oversee.

During Production, DPs direct the camera crew, blocks the shots, directs the camera and lighting crews with particular focus on composition and movements, and reviews each day's unedited footage. Not only do they have the largest crew on set, they're also in continual communication with the director and production designer to make sure everyone is on the same page in terms of a visual style. They also attend any rehearsals to adjust the camera in response to a gesture, action, or change in blocking.

In post-production, a DP will and can consult on color, be in the driver's seat and be the director in the editing process and sometimes, the DP will be brought in to help choose takes or consult on color-grading.

Skills of a Director of Photography aka DP

1. Must be able to "track the journey of light"
2. Have a strong technical knowledge of camera equipment and lighting. They must master the interplay between light, lenses, and locations, as well as camera operation and techniques.

Professional Director of Photographers to Know: **Patrick A. Stewart** *("Curb Your Enthusiasm")*

27

DISTRIBUTION EXECUTIVE

Distribution Executives get films into cinemas and TV dramas onto TV screens and onto other streaming platforms like Amazon or Netflix.

In film, distribution executives go to film markets where they look at films and acquire them from production companies or sales agents. They negotiate for the rights to release them. These deals cover a set period and include agreements about promotion, classification of the film and any edits allowed. Distribution executives then pitch the film to exhibitors (usually cinemas). They deliver the film materials to them and plan the release, including how to market the film, targeting the film's core audience to bring in the most profit. How well a film does when it first opens in the cinema has a big impact on the rest of its release cycle.

In TV drama, distributors play a slightly different role. Big budget dramas are usually financed by a combination of TV channels and distribution companies. The distribution company will advance money to produce the drama against the right to sell broadcast rights in the program for a set time period in specific countries. They might also be responsible for any merchandising or publishing spinoffs. Distribution executives are often essential to the financing of the TV drama in development (prior to production) and can also play an important part in helping form the content of new dramas.

Skills of a Distribution Executive
- Good at Watching Film: Have a passion for and wide knowledge of the industry, critically analyze scripts and production packages, know film festivals and how they work
- Market Knowledge: identify and understand the core audience for a film, know how to excite them, research box office and viewing figures, be aware of cultural trends including past statistics, predict what will be successful
- Industry Knowledge: have an in-depth understanding of the film and TV drama industry, including the production process, how to turn talent into commercial success, convert master materials from film makers into exhibition formats
- Negotiation: be good at selling, execute deals on an international and global level, understand contractual agreements
- Finance: manage a budget and handle accounts, be very well organized
- Networking: communicate well with a wide range of people in the film industry

28

DOLLY GRIP

A Dolly Grip is a technician in film who operates a camera dolly: a wheeled platform that moves a camera on a track to create smooth, horizontal camera movements. Dolly grips are responsible for ensuring that the dolly's movement is seamless during shots, which can help create fluid scenes. Dolly grips also build and maintain other special equipment used on a film set, such as cranes or jibs. They place, level, and move the dolly track, and then push and pull the dolly, often with a camera operator and camera assistant riding along. Dolly grips should be technically minded and have knowledge of camera and lighting equipment, construction, carpentry, mechanics, electrical systems, and wiring. They should also be in good physical condition, as they'll likely spend a large part of their day carrying heavy equipment and climbing ladders.

29

EDITOR

A film Editor is responsible for assembling a film from start to finish, working closely with the director and producers to create a final version that represents the filmmakers' vision. This process involves cutting together raw footage into a logical sequence, and can include picture editing, VFX, dialogue editing, sound design, SFX editing, and music editing. Film editors play a dynamic role in the filmmaking process, and their skills can be crucial to the success of a film. They must creatively manipulate the layers of images, story, dialogue, music, pacing, and actors' performances to effectively "re-imagine" and rewrite the film.

This can include selecting only the most quality shots, removing unnecessary frames, and editing scenes in non-story order to create a continuous and enjoyable whole. Editors may also be involved in the pre-production process, working closely with the director to decide how to make the most of the script. Depending on the scale of production, they may also organize footage into a system that supports post-production efficiency, or even visit shooting locations to check in on progress and begin cutting right away.

Some say that film editing is comparable to literary editing, where an editor might work with an author to transform a manuscript into a finished version.

Professional Editor to Know: **Aziza Ngozi** ("BMF") Season III

30

ENVIRONMENT ARTIST

Environment Artists create the computer-generated places in which actors move. They make galaxies, lunar landscapes, and desecrated cities – any environment that it's too difficult to film in real life. They create the 3D environments using modelling and sculpting software. They often work from a brief delivered to them in the form of 2D, or, sometimes, 3D digital art, produced by a concept artist. Or they might work from reference materials, such as photographs or line drawing sketches, which can be scanned into 3D software.

They first create a 'wireframe', commonly referred to as a 'mesh', of the environment. This looks like a series of overlapping lines (or interconnected polygon shapes) in the shape of the intended 3D environment. Usually, the more detailed the environment is (the more polygons it is made up of), the more photorealistic it looks.

From the mesh, they can further sculpt the environment to more closely resemble what's intended. They use digital tools, such as sculpting brushes, and a physical graphics pen and tablet to do this.

Environment artists work at an early stage of the CGI and 3D part of their VFX pipeline. The 3D environments that they produce can then move on to be given texture and be lit.

Environment artists work for VFX companies or studios or as freelancers. Smaller VFX companies or studios may not distinguish between environment, modelling, and texturing artist roles, and instead advertise for one modelling artist position, involving all roles.

Here are a few tools used by professionals:

- 3D modelling
- Sculpting and Painting Software (Blender, 3ds Max, Maya, Mudbox, ZBrush, Substance Painter)
- Graphics Software (Adobe After Effects, Dreamweaver, Illustrator, Photoshop)

31

FILM ARCHIVIST

Film Archivists are the librarians of the film and TV drama industry. They work for large film studios (Pinewood) for broadcasters like ITV and the BBC and for organizations like the British Film Institute.

They work with old and new films, restoring and digitizing the films of the past. A lot of companies find themselves with ageing archives of difficult-to-store film reels and videotapes that are becoming obsolete. An archivist is responsible for scanning or digitizing these tapes into a digital medium to make them easier to access in the future with a planned migration for long term storage.

Example: Whenever a British film is made, the final raw mastered media, proxy files, script, production schedule and stills are sent to the British Film Institute and sometimes the archives of the broadcaster or production company. The archivist will catalogue it and put metadata into the digital file so that it can be found later.

Archivists work with all kinds of formats such as film reels, videotapes, DVDs, CDs, QuickTime's, and other digital files. They also work with all kinds of people, getting requests for footage that the archivist must retrieve quickly and efficiently.

32

Finance Controller

Finance Controllers oversee the team that makes sure a production is legally and financially managed. They have a high level of authority, to the extent they can even override a producer with their decisions.

They are often employed by the studio, financier or broadcaster that's investing in, or commissioning, the production. They are accountable to the people who have come up with the cash, so it's their job to make sure the film is completed within budget and the money is spent properly.

Skills of a Good Finance Controller

- Accountancy: Keep books meticulously, know Inland Revenue regulations and insurance
- Use Finance Software such as Movie Magic Budgeting or other finance packages
- Knowledge of Film Production
- Communication: Listen to and be understood by everyone from producers, financiers, production accountants and cashiers
- Negotiation: Be able to influence and persuade
- Discretion: Be able to maintain confidences

33

GAFFER

A Gaffer oversees the electrical department on a production. Working closely with the director of photography, the gaffer's job is to help execute the DP's vision by designing the lighting. Gaffers are also heavily involved during pre-production, studying the script and meeting with the director, DP, and key grip to map out the aesthetics of the film. They must also communicate with producers and production managers to determine the project's electric and crew budgets and hire their best boy electric.

A strong skill to have as a good gaffer is have a "cool head."

The primary responsibilities of a gaffer include:

- Figuring out the proper light placement
- Selecting and managing the electrical equipment and lighting instruments for each shot, including colored gels and filters
- Running cables
- Setting up generators
- Overseeing a team of lighting technicians and maintaining safety.
- Monitors the lighting conditions during the shoot to ensure the set's ambiance is up to snuff.

"You could walk into a job like 'Mission: Impossible,' 'Transformers,' '13 Hours'— these jobs can be overwhelming. On paper, they look immensely unachievable. I've stood there on some days and felt really overwhelmed—sweaty palms, nervousness. But you gotta break it down; you gotta look at the smaller parts. If you break it down into small chunks of work with your team, with your rigging crew, anything is achievable. You only learn that by working."

Martin Smith (Professional Gaffer to Know)

34

GRAPHIC DESIGNER

A film Graphic Designer is responsible for all graphical elements in a film or television show, including typography, illustration, patterns, and set pieces. They work closely with other departments, such as art, set decoration, props, painters, and construction.

35

GREENSPERSON AKA GREENSMAN, GREENSPERSON, NURSERYMAN, GREENSKEEPER, GREENS FOREMAN

This professional is any production personnel on a film set who is responsible for obtaining and taking care of anything "green" or natural used in the film production. This may include plants, grass, trees, flowers, and other various landscaping materials like rocks, gravel, sand, etc. They are considered part of the Art Department. The role includes the use of artificial materials such as simulated rocks, silk flowers and items representing greens, such as camouflage netting. The greensperson functions as a participant in the filmmaking process as an extension of the art department during set construction and in conjunction with the camera department during filming. In addition to set construction, greenspeople often work "on set" assisting the camera team and other departments in adjusting the set to the changing demands of different camera positions and lighting setups, as requested by the creative leaders.

Duties of a Greensperson range from tending to plant nursery operations (watering, fertilizing, transplanting grass, flowers, bushes, etc.) through to the artful crafting of vines, trees, flowers and the like using cut living material and/or various simulated materials.

36

GRIP

A Grip is a technician who sets up, operates, and maintains the rigging and equipment that supports the camera (i.e., dollies, cranes, tracks, jibs, tripods, process trailers, etc.) and lighting (stands, diffusers, nets, etc.) to achieve the director and cinematographer's desired shot. Under the direction of the Best Boy Electric (who reports to the key grip), a grip builds, lifts, moves, and adjusts the production gear that helps a scene feel alive. Often, a grip builds the lights.

37

ILLUSTRATOR

An Illustrator is an artist who creates two-dimensional images for various companies and industries, such as film, TV, commercials', documentaries, development, pre-production, technical designs, pre-sales, and advertising. The illustrator will use various techniques to create effects, like the simplicity of black and white, the richness of color, or the use of light and shadows. An illustrator will usually begin by sketching out a draft of the images they want to make. Once they have an idea of the quantity and the general outline of the whole project, they begin working on drawing each illustration. Illustrators can work from pencil and paper or digitally on the computer. They can choose the medium that works best for their style and their client's needs. Every illustrator has excellent drawing skills so that they can produce all kinds of images and designs.

Tools Used by Illustrator(s)

1. Hand sketches and a great deal to do with Photoshop and/or 3D modeling. Hand sketches are often used simply as a conversational tool between the illustrator and production designer.

2. Adobe Illustrator & Cad Tools

Adobe Illustrator is a great tool for the film illustrator, particularly if you're involved early enough in the design process that you are working out rough plans and elevations along with the sketches. With a really useful plug-in called CAD tools, Illustrator becomes a great CAD drawing and drafting tool. CAD tools is a whole CAD drafting package that allows you to do just about any kind of drawing… plans, elevations, or isometrics in scale. You have all the advantages of working in Illustrator, with CAD capabilities to boot. And there are add-on libraries of standard textures and symbols.

3. ADOBE PHOTOSHOP (ADOBE CS5)

Photoshop is the powerhouse of illustration. Whether its hand drawing, digital sketch or 3D rendering, you can turn hand illustration into a color rendering by doing a very finished pencil rendering, which you can then scan into Photoshop.

4. 3D Modeling

38

INFORMATION TECHNOLOGY/TECHNOLOGIST (IT)

Information technology (IT) is a broad field that involves the development, maintenance, and use of computer systems and networks. IT professionals' study, design, develop, implement, support, and manage computer-based information systems, including both software applications and computer hardware.

Some examples of IT jobs include:

- Web developer: Creates the look and technical aspects of a website
- Network administrator: Ensures the computer network for an organization is secure, and runs smoothly
- Software developer: Designs computer applications or programs
- Identifies problems with applications or programs and reports defects
- Tester: Identifies problems with applications or programs and reports defects

Professional IT to Know: Alex Ankrah *(Add1 Technologies)*

39

Intimacy Coordinator

Intimacy Coordinators work with actors and film production teams to ensure that intimate scenes are carried out safely, respectfully, and consensually. Intimacy covers a far wider umbrella than just sex scenes and kissing. For example, intimacy coordinators may also help actors feel comfortable in a close physical space. They may suggest to the actors when to move, how many beats each movement is, and when the movement is closed or done. Intimacy coordinators are used on most major television shows, and intimacy direction is now an integral part of live performance in regional theater, opera, and dance, as well as on Broadway.

Professional Intimacy Coordinator to Know: **Katherine O'Keefe** *("Bridgerton" Season III)*

40

<hr>

KEY HAIRSTYLIST

The Key Hairstylist oversees creating and styling every character's hair on set. They are the head of the hair team within the hair and makeup department, and he/she is involved in designing and execution, including hiring a team to cover every single actor on set, extras included. During both preproduction and shooting days, the key hairstylist often collaborates with the wardrobe department to ensure the project maintains a cohesive aesthetic.

"We provide the look for the film, as far as the hair goes,"

LaWanda Pierre, *key hairstylist on "Uncut Gems" and "BlacKkKlansman," told Backstage. "Everyone has to look like they're not in a Halloween costume but like real people, and we can't have one person's appearance mess it up."*

Professional Key Hairstylist to Know: **Kim Berry** *(Prince)*

During preproduction

The key hairstylist analyzes the script to create and test designs, cuts, and coloring for the cast's hair. This process often involves compiling reference images, particularly if the project calls for a specific time or follows a historical figure. They also hire the team of hairstylists and hair assistants who will be executing much of the day-to-day styling on set.

On set

The key hairstylist is present during shooting to maintain the actors' hair between takes, as well as execute the hairstyling themselves for any of the main cast. As the head of their team, they oversee delegating any responsibilities having to do with the project's hair looks. Often, the key hairstylist keeps photos of all hair and wigs for continuity in the event reshoots are necessary.

Question– *"How was it that you came to be involved with hair for on-camera projects?"*

"I'm a hairstylist. I was working in a hair salon. I've been doing hair for about 10 years now, but I've only been in the film and television industry for about 6 years. I met Spike on "Red Hook Summer," a film he did a few years ago. It was a small film shot in 18 days, and I had a client who would come to me and get her hair done. She happened to be an actress, and she was in this film. What happened was, Spike had a hair stylist who wasn't available every day of the 18 days to shoot. So, I came to do my particular actor's hair and then ended up doing everyone because she wasn't available to finish the job. From then, he really liked me, and he liked my work so he asked me to do "Sweet Blood of Jesus" right after that. He called me personally and asked me to do it, and of course I was honored and floored."

– **LaWanda Pierre** via Backstage

41

KEY GRIP

A Key Grip is a senior role on a film set, responsible for managing the grip department and all non-electrical equipment. They work closely with the director of photography (DP) to ensure that shots are captured as intended and that everything runs smoothly. Depending on the production's size and budget, a key grip may have an assistant called a "best boy" or "best girl" to help them manage the grips. Here are some of the tasks a key grip may perform:

- Equipment: Assess what equipment is needed for each location, coordinate its transportation and setup, and keep track of it before, during, and after the show

- Camera: Collaborate with the DP to arrange the camera's movement and positioning

- Lighting: Work with the gaffer to execute the DP's plan for lighting

- Safety: Ensure on-set safety

- Supervision: Manage other grips and electric crew members, and assign grips to tasks

- Builds and Rigs: Oversee the construction of platforms, rigging, and other equipment

42

KEY MAKEUP ARTIST

The Key Makeup artist oversees and leads the makeup department. They are responsible for planning makeup designs for the leading and supporting cast, including special effects makeup or prosthetic work, and hiring assistants to recreate these looks on the rest of the cast. During production, the key makeup artist applies the daily makeup to the principal actors and assigns tasks to their team and keeps track of continuity. They're also on set for touch-ups between takes.

"I kind of look at the makeup like music. Like on a film or TV, the music [can] emotionally elevate a scene [or] can make a scene go from like zero to sixty in terms of emotion," says "I aim to do something similar. If the makeup I'm doing is not enhancing the story, then it's not doing its job."

Professional Key Makeup Artist to Know: **Doniella Davy** *("Euphoria," +*
"Moonlight")

43

LIGHTING ARTIST (VFX)

Lighting Artists enable depth and realism to be added to a computer-generated (CG) scene through lighting, just as a Director of Photography (DofP) does in a live-action film. They adjust the color, placement, and intensity of CG lights to create atmosphere, add realism and depth. Using reference photos taken on set or location, they match the illumination of virtual 3D objects to the look of the on-set production and cinematography.

Lighting a shot requires a blend of artistry and scientific knowledge of how light falls on objects. It also involves reflecting the look and style set out by the director of the film or TV programmer. This can create technical challenges.

The role of the lighting artist varies depending on the size of the VFX studio. In larger studios, lighting artists light the shots while a lighting technical director works with the pipeline technical director to overcome the technical challenges and create the software tools that the lighting artist needs. In other studios, those two roles are combined, so the lighting artist needs considerable technical skills as well as artistic ones.

44

Lighting Board Operator also known as the "Light Op" or "Board Op"

The Light Board Operator is the electrician who operates and may even program the light board. They are considered part of the "Electrics" Department or LX Department. All non-design elements of lighting will be handled by the LX Department, i.e. electricians. Light board operators mainly are responsible for decoding the light designer's ideas from paper to opening night ready. In some cases, the light board operator is also the light designer.

This position carries out all the cues for the production, essentially functioning as a "human light switch", from a light board console. The scope of the cues can differ depending on the production needs; examples like cutting all lights so a spotlight can shine on a single actor or dimming lights at the start of a production or even a complex scene incorporating several rapid-fire lighting cues paired to certain sounds. Many cues are even programmed by light board operators, a skill that is necessary for the modern-day light board operator.

Light board operators also must be attentive, being ready for any quick adjustments needed during a live production, where failures or improv can occur at any time. This profession is also not limited to just theaters, any event where lighting is a critical part of the experience, such as concerts or live events, expect to see a light board operator behind the scenes.

Professional Lighting Crew Chief/Production Electrician to Know – **James Jones** (*Olivia Rodrigo, Nickelback, Bon Jovi, Foo Fighters*)

45

LIGHTING TECHNICIAN

A Lighting Technician on a film set uses their technical skills to set up and operate lighting equipment to create the right atmosphere for a scene and evoke a response from the audience. They work under the direction of the gaffer or chief lighting technician, who takes direction from the cinematographer.

46

LINE PRODUCER

A Line Producer is a type of film or television producer who is the head of the production office management personnel during daily operations of a feature film, advertisement film, television film, or TV program. They are responsible for human resources and handling any problems that come up during production. Line producers also manage scheduling and the budget of a motion picture, as well as day-to-day physical aspects of the film production.

47

LOCATION ENGINEER

Location Engineers set up the studios and technology needed to broadcast TV programs from all over the world. This could be at an international conference for climate change, the aftermath of an earthquake, the tennis at Wimbledon, a big political announcement at Downing Street or a war zone like Ukraine. This job combines technology while being at the heart of big events.

A location engineer needs to be able to drive and operate broadcast vehicles such as satellite-link trucks – vans with satellite dishes on the roof that send footage back to the studio at home. They also need to be able to set up links to the newsroom or studio over the internet. They find solutions to colleagues' technical problems and use the equipment they have with them – however limited – to get programs, or the latest news report, onto our TVs, laptops, and phones.

48

Location Manager

A Location Manager is a key figure in the pre-production and production stages of film, TV, or commercial production. They are responsible for finding, securing, and supervising locations that align with the director and production designer's vision for the film. The location's impact on the film's look, feel, and story is important. Location managers' responsibilities include:

- Researching Locations: Based on scripts and discussions with other department heads, location managers look for places that evoke the world of the film.
- Securing Locations: Negotiating contracts and obtaining permits
- Managing Logistics: Coordinating parking, trash removal, and any required police activity, to name a few.

49

LOGGERS

If you were about to edit an hour-long unscripted TV show, you might find yourself faced with hours and hours of footage and wonder where on earth to start. Loggers watch all the rushes (raw footage) and create a detailed document describing what footage is on which tape. They 'log' the timecodes as they go, sometimes using specific software to do this. This enables editors to find what they need to cut together a program.

Loggers make notes of the best footage, key themes and story arcs, sometimes transcribing parts of interviews. They note tone, as well as which bits of footage are usable, and which are not.

They can work in production or post-production. During production, loggers record action as it happens. They might use a phone or tablet or take notes using pen and paper. In post-production, loggers work using footage that has already been recorded, often in an edit suite. Loggers sometimes also act as archivists, hunting out existing footage that the program needs. They deliver these to the post-production team.

Depending on the production, you may be supplied with materials needed by the production manager. Below are a few tools you might use once you are working:

- Pen and paper
- A phone or tablet
- Logging software
  - Live Logger
  - Timecode+

In an edit suite or working from home, you may need:

- Microsoft Office
- Blackbird
- Avid Interplay

50

MATCHMOVE ARTISTS

Matchmove Artists match computer-generated (CG) scenes with shots from live-action footage so the two can be convincingly combined. They recreate live-action backgrounds (plates) on a computer in a way that mirrors the camera on the set in every way, including lens distortion. They do this by tracking the camera movements to make sure the real and virtual scenes appear from the same perspective. Sometimes matchmove artists go to the film set to take measurements and put-up tracking markers. Then they use these markers to track the camera movement and work out the relevant coordinates in the 3D scene. They do this using 3D tracking programs like Maya or 3DEqualizer. Matchmove artists also do body and object tracking, using markers to recreate the movements of people, vehicles or other objects in CG. The motion files created (camera, object or body track) are then passed on to other departments via the VFX pipeline, so that, eventually, they can be seamlessly combined by the compositor.

Matchmove artists are highly accurate and meticulous in their work. It needs to be pixel perfect, so they need an eye for detail. If the CG and live-action movements are not lining up perfectly, they must find a way to fix this.

51

MODELLING ARTIST

Modelling Artists create characters, weapons, plants, and animals on a computer in 3D.

Process for a Modelling Artist

They start with a brief, which might be 2D or 3D art produced by a concept artist. Or they can work from reference materials, such as photographs or line drawing sketches, which can be scanned into 3D software. They first create a 'wireframe', commonly referred to as a 'mesh,' of the object. This looks like a series of overlapping lines in the shape of the intended 3D model. From the mesh, they can sculpt the model of the object to closely resemble what's intended. They use digital tools, such as sculpting brushes, and a physical graphics pen and tablet.

Modelling artists work at an early stage of the CG and 3D part of the VFX pipeline. The 3D models that they produce can then move on to be animated, given texture and lit. If a modelling artist specializes in creating a specific type of 3D model, for instance, characters, then they may refer to themselves as a character artist. In this case, they will likely create both the models and textures for characters.

TOOLS – 3D Modelling and Sculpting Software *such as*

- Blender
- 3ds Max
- Mudbox
- ZBrush

52

MOTIONS GRAPHICS DESIGNER

Motion Graphic Designers is one of the most interesting jobs, in my eyes. They are essential in the making of any TV show, film, video game or commercial. They might be required to create the opening titles for a new TV series or a sequence that explains the growth of a deadly virus for a documentary. They could be asked to design the style of name captions on a chat show or create stylized graphic elements such as an animated chart showing the number of medal winners in the Olympics.

They are often called upon to create an entire "look" for a new series. For example: for a talent show or quiz game that means providing the opening titles, logos, name captions and closing credits, as well as working with the color palette and design of the set so that the program has a coherent, easily identifiable look. This is particularly important if the series format is to be sold around the world. It's important to design graphics that work well not only on television or in the cinema, but also on social media, in print media and even on T-shirts and other merchandise.

Motion graphics designers need to be able to assess a production brief and understand and work with those requirements during pre-production through to design, production itself and final post.

Recently there's been a move for motion designers to work on VR (virtual reality) elements for films and studio productions, using green screens and 3D graphic software. Some designers work within production. For example, news graphics are usually prepared just before a story goes out, while on films they may need to design something that's part of a film set, such as a prop like a newspaper or poster. However, only motion graphics designers work within the post-production family and a vast amount of the work they do comes after the program has been filmed or recorded.

A successful motion graphics designer will have the opportunity to create sequences that become legendary, perhaps by producing the opening titles of a long-running sports program, film title sequence or even the totalizer in a much-loved charity telethon.

Professional Motion Graphics Designer to Know: Annie Atkins (Academy Awardee for Best Production Design for Wes Anderson's The Grand Budapest Hotel)

Learn More About Annie Atkins in "The Secret World of Graphic Design for Filmmaking"

53

MUSIC CONTRACTOR

Music Contractors are best known in the film and television industries responsible for finding the session players and conductor to record a film score, television score, or a show's theme. They can also work in the theater industry—finding pit orchestra musicians for a play, musical, or opera—or in the live and recorded music industries, where they might hire backup singers and touring musicians for a recording artist or music director or connect a songwriter recording an album with skilled session musicians.

Professional Music Contractors to Know: **Steve Epting** *(Beyoncé, Kanye West)*

54

MUSIC COORDINATOR

A Music Coordinator in film & television is responsible for managing the music selection process for a production, including selecting a soundtrack, securing rights, and hiring composers. They also work with other professionals to ensure the music fits the intended audience and budget. Here are some of the responsibilities of a music coordinator in film:

Music Coordinators may...

- Research relevant music to match the audience.
- Secure rights
- Negotiate and acquire synchronization rights for the show's music.
- Hire composers
- Hire composers to write original music for the soundtrack.
- Work with contractors to ensure the right number and type of musicians are hired for the project. They may also assist with musicians' union contracts and arrangements.
- Work with composers or songwriters to establish a realistic budget and manage the music creation and recording processes to stay within that budget.
- Track schedule details, such as shoot dates for music scenes and final mix stage dates. They also log contact information for key players, read scripts and note music moments, and keep track of changes to songs between different versions of the film.
- Create cue sheets and Work with music editors and supervisors to create and deliver cue sheets.
- Ensure correct royalty distribution
- May ensure that the film's music royalties are distributed correctly.

55

MUSIC DATA ANALYST

A Music Data Analyst works with music industry executives to use music data to make predictions on future music trends. A music industry analyst could be working to discover the next hot artist, identifying core demographics for a concert venue or festival, or using sales data to identify a label artist's next career move.

56

MUSIC EDITOR

Music Editors are responsible for all the music in a film or TV production, including the soundtrack and any music created by the composer and often act as a bridge between the sound and picture teams. The extent of their role varies considerably depending on the type of production concerned.

On a medium-budget film, they usually start work while the film is being edited. They work with the Director to decide on the purpose of the music, find a style to suit the story and mark the points in the film where music is required. Then they develop the temporary score. Music editors then work closely with a composer, who is usually appointed by the director, and who composes the music using the temp score as a template. The temp score is also used by the film editors to achieve the right tempo with the cut.

They attend all recording sessions, helping with any revisions and design a 'click track' which is used to help the musicians achieve synchronization with the movie. Working with a specialist music mixer, they create different mixes, lay down the tracks and fit them exactly to the picture, ready for the final mix or dub.

One of the final tasks for music editors (and often times Music Supervisor) on films is preparing the cue sheet - a detailed breakdown of all the music featured on soundtracks. This is sent to the Performing Rights Society and all exhibitors so that royalties can be paid every time the film is screened.

Skills of a Music Editor
- Music: Know the history and construction of music and create themes quickly under the pressure of deadlines.
- Understanding Film Production: Appreciate the process and techniques of making films, know how music affects images and adds drama.
- Collaboration: Listen to the director, translate the vision into music, be flexible, communicate the vision with the editor, composer and other musicians
- Using Software: Produce electronic scores using technology such as ProTools, use editing and mixing software
- Business: Know people in the music, film and TV industries.

57

Music Supervisor

A Music Supervisor is a person who combines music and visual media. According to The Guild of Music Supervisors, a music supervisor is "a qualified professional who oversees all music related aspects of film, television, advertising, video games and other existing or emerging visual media platforms as required."

Professional Music Supervisors to Know: **Ashley Davis** *("That Damn Michael Che" Show on HBO MAX) and* **Ashley Neumeister** *("The Game" on Paramount+)*

58

Office Production Assistant (PA)

An Office Production Assistant (PA) is an entry-level role on a film or television production that involves supporting the production office and its staff. They work closely with the production coordinator and producer to complete administrative tasks and other duties.

Some of the tasks an Office PA might perform include:

- Answering phones
- Managing paperwork
- Running errands
- Ordering lunch and coffee
- Maintaining craft services
- Scheduling meetings and table reads
- Sending and receiving paperwork from set
- Making signs for the office
- Setting up meeting rooms
- Preparing for special occasions

Office PAs are usually based in the production office, which can be located on the studio lot or elsewhere. They should be familiar with call sheets, scripts, schedules, and other relevant documents.

59

PAYROLL

Payroll in film is the process of paying a production's cast and crew members, and it can also refer to the list of employees and the amount they are paid. Film payroll differs from payroll for other businesses in a few ways:

- Short-term
- Film payroll is cyclical and temporary, with employees paid per shoot, which can last a few weeks or months. For each new project, the entire payroll process must be repeated from scratch.
- Requires knowledge of unions
- For union productions, the payroll company needs to be familiar with the contracts of the various guilds and union locals that represent the production's employees. These contracts can include collective bargaining agreements that outline minimum wage and working conditions for each crew member and talent. Most film productions use a payroll company to handle payroll, which can free up time for the production team to focus on other aspects of the project.
- Payroll companies are also responsible for other tasks, such as: Handling tax paperwork, helping to get security deposits back from unions, dealing with unemployment, and reporting new hires.

To learn more about Payroll, visit **The 10 Best Entertainment Payroll Companies**

60

Photo/Picture Editor

A Photo Editor's job description may include the following responsibilities:

- Managing projects
- May hire and manage photographers for projects and assign projects to meet the organization's needs.
- Selecting and reviewing images
- May review and select photos for publication, promotion, or other purposes. They may also choose the most appropriate photos for a story and edit them to meet the company's aesthetic standards.
- Editing images
- Photo editors may use imaging software like Photoshop to manipulate and enhance images, such as resizing, retouching, and color correcting stock images. They may also arrange images in a suitable layout.
- Photo editors may collaborate with photographers, editors, managers, and clients to ensure visuals align with brand and messaging, and to meet client objectives. They may also provide photographers with instructions, feedback, and advice.
- Staying current
- Photo editors may stay up to date on industry trends and best practices.

Other responsibilities may include - Handling photography paperwork, Time management, Digital design, and Communication.

Photo editors may work in journalism, marketing, entertainment, and other content publishing industries, either within a company or as freelancers. To excel in this role, they may need strong photo editing skills, a thorough knowledge of computer imaging and photographic techniques, and a creative mind with an eye for detail.

Professional Photo Editor to Know: **Joan Sobel** (*"Kill Bill: Vol. 1"*)

61

Picture Car Coordinator

A Picture Car Coordinator is a specialized technician who works on set with cars in films and TV shows. They are responsible for ensuring that motor vehicles in a scene meet the director's needs, which can include scientific and mechanical tasks.

He/she oversees the modification, movement, usage, and repair of vehicles appearing in a film. They must ensure that rigid timetables of film productions will not be interrupted by vehicle mishaps like a car failing to start. In addition, picture car coordinators maintain open communications with specialized vehicle builders to be aware of any problems that may arise or parts that need replacing. This makes it easier to ensure that they have mechanics and components available to fix an issue quickly, so it doesn't affect the film.

In the movie "Argo," director Ben Affleck asked picture car coordinator **Ted Moser** to make a Unimog go 70 miles per hour, even though the vehicle normally only goes 37 miles per hour. Moser solved the problem by combining the body of a Ram Charger with the body of the Unimog.

Professional Picture Car Coordinator to Know: **Ted Moser** (*"Now You See Me"* and *"Argo"*)

62

POSTPRODUCTION SUPERVISOR/PRODUCER

One of my favorite people to work with in television and film, is a Postproduction Supervisor. In this position, you are the glue to all members of a production, and you tie it all together. He or She is responsible for supervising the post-production process: pulling the final project together, making sure deadlines are met, overseeing reshoots and visual effects (particularly to make sure a project doesn't go over budget in the editing process), editing, printing, delivery, and maintaining communication between producers, editors, and companies work has been outsourced to (like film labs, FX studios, etc.). Ideally, they will also consult with the team about expectations and budgets during and/in pre-production. In this position, you must maintain the integrity of a film or television show by overseeing color correction and visual effects, handling quality control, and managing billing and paperwork.

Professional Postproduction Supervisors to Know - **Kevin Murray** *("American Horror Story")*

"I originally learned about Postproduction from a Executive Producer in the Reality/Documentary field. She noticed some of the work I was doing and thought I'd be a good fit for the career. Originally, I was working in Finance, and only dabbled in Production and Post-like activities at the time. I made the move to Post a few years later after taking a side job as a Teleprompter Operator for various MTV shows which opened the doors to the industry for me." - Kevin Murray

Educational Background of Kevin Murray:

- University/College - University of Washington
- Studied Business and Finance
- Favorite Project *(so far)* – "Designated Survivor" (NETFLIX)
- Skills as a Postproduction Supervisor - Landed a job as a Teleprompter Op and then freelanced as a Production Assistant.
  - Having basic office
  - Verbal and tech skills

63

PRINT PRODUCTION ASSOCIATE/ASSISTANT

As a Print Production Associate/Assistant, your job is to work with clients to create, schedule and produce their print products. You operate finishing equipment like paper cutters, lamination machines, and hole punchers.

64

PRODUCTION ACCOUNTANT

Production Accountants do all the things accountants do, but they do it on film locations amidst the buzz and creativity of making a movie. They calculate finances, work out the cost of a production, talk to the completion guarantor (an insurance policy to make sure the film is delivered on time and on budget) and control the cash flow, or spending.

In pre-production, production accountants help the producers and production managers prepare budgets and estimated final cost reports.

During production, they oversee all payments, manage payroll and provide daily or weekly cost reports. They also produce cost forecasts to evaluate the impact of any production changes.

Production accountants prepare a statement of account showing all income and expenditure for the producer or production company and the financiers. They may also have to arrange an independent audit. Depending on how the production is financed, they may also have to deal with bank finance and completion guarantors.

On larger productions, production accountants may work with Finance Controllers who are often permanently employed by studios and broadcasters. Production accountants are usually freelancers.

65

PRODUCTION ASSISTANT (PA)

A Production Assistant (PA) is an entry-level position that assists with general tasks on a film, television, commercial or digital media production. Some PAs work in the production department with the First or Second Assistant Director to provide support and communication to multiple departments. PAs may also work in the production office or in other departments, such as the art, wardrobe, animation, development, or locations department.

Production Assistant provides support on set where it's needed, doing a huge variety of tasks throughout a shoot. A PAs job can include moving equipment, managing background actors, escorting actors to and from their trailers, delivering hard drives of footage to editors, handing out scripts and shooting schedules, organizing paperwork, cleaning up the set, and taking coffee orders, among other things. Depending on the tasks, a PA can be stationed in the various locations below:

Set PA - Set PAs work on set under the guidance of the Assistant Directors and will interact with most departments. Set PAs help with the entirety of a production day, from set up through breakdown. Responsibilities include maintaining base camp, distributing paperwork, running errands, making sure no one walks into a shot, managing the craft service area, helping with company moves, managing crowds, extras registration, loading / unloading equipment and other duties as assigned.

Office PA - An Office PA works in the production office and provides traditional clerical support including answering phones, data entry, managing paperwork and running errands.

Art Department PA - Art Department PAs assist the art department with office duties, running errands and may assist with construction of props or set dressing.

Wardrobe PA - Wardrobe PAs support the wardrobe department and assist the costumer with labeling costumes, organizing costumes for laundry service, costume collection and running errands as assigned.

Location PA - Location PAs assist the location department with location management and maintenance. Some of the duties include distributing location agreements and neighbor notification letters, setting up signs directing crew to set, creating and distributing maps to locations, distributing notification letters, running errands and cleaning a location after wrap.

66

PRODUCTION BUYER

A Production Buyer, also known as a prop's buyer, is a member of a film or TV drama's art department who purchases and hires props for a production's sets. They work closely with set decorators and production designers to ensure the props meet the needs of the set's look and action. Production buyers are responsible for many tasks, including budgeting, sourcing, organizing, communication Collecting and returning assets on time according to the shooting schedule.

67

PRODUCTION DESIGNER

Production Designers often specialize in film, television, or theater, but there is some overlap. A production designer is responsible for the visual concept of a film, including the overall aesthetic and look and feel of the story. They work closely with the director and producer to bring the director's vision to life, and their designs help immerse the audience in the story.

As a production designer, you'll identify a design style for sets, locations, graphics, props, lighting, camera angles and costumes, while working closely with the director and producer. Once the concept is decided, you'll usually appoint and manage an art department, which includes a design and construction team. A production designer is responsible for the overall look of a project by taking the script, the Director's vision, and the producer's plan and budget and turning them into a visual story. The production designer is the head of the Art Department. Their work also touches multiple other departments and runs through all three stages of production: preproduction, principal photography, and postproduction. In short, the production designer has a hand in every visual element of a project.

"The production designer is supposed to design the movie. We find the look, the color, the texture, the location of the movie and we choose where and how to shoot it, either onstage or on location, and in which country. You're the first one to be hired on a movie, and the one helping the production decide everything about its look."

Jean-Vincent Puzos ("The Lost City of Z," and "Jungle Cruise")

Degrees to Consider - Film or Theater Production or Graphic Design.

Professional Production Designers to Know: **Hannah Beachler** *("Black Panther")*

68

PRODUCTION HEALTH & SAFETY SUPERVISOR

As a Production Safety Supervisor, your focus revolves around health and safety meetings in TV, film, and commercial productions. Specializing in film, TV, commercials, and live events, you bring expertise in conducting thorough risk assessments, implementing comprehensive health and safety protocols, and fostering a vigilant set environment. In this position, you oversee the well-being of the cast and crew.

69

PRODUCTION SECRETARY

A Production Secretary, also known as a Production Assistant, is responsible for the smooth running of a film or television production's office. They work in the production management department and may be based in the office, on location, or with the director.

Production Secretaries provide administrative and organiza-tional support to the production coordinator and production manager. Their duties include Managing paperwork, maintaining logs, scheduling, communication, running errands and problem-solving.

70

Property Master (Prop Master)

A Property Master, also known as a prop master, is a member of a film production's art department who manages all props used in the production. Props are movable items that actors use during a performance, such as hats, guns, wine glasses, or lightsabers. A property master's responsibilities include:

- Acquiring props: Purchasing, manufacturing, or otherwise obtaining props
- Preparing props: Making sure props are ready for each shoot
- Organizing props: Storing and transporting props
- Researching props: Drawing up property lists
- Managing the props department: Supervising and directing prop makers, runners, and other assistants
- Maintaining Continuity: Working with the script supervisor to ensure set continuity
- Managing Logistics: Providing props and resources to the production designer that fit with the director's vision

Professional Prop Masters to Know: **Sean Davis** (*"Ironheart" & "The Have and the Have Nots"*)

"My sister, Ashley Davis, used to hear me complain about being an actor. I could not fathom how anyone or her, for that matter, could learn so many lines in a short amount of time. So, my sister set up a meeting with Mark Swinton at Tyler Perry Studios. On June 7, 2017, Mark met with me. He looked at a resume that I didn't really have. Mark honored my education (University of South Florida) and because I graduated, it gave Mark a reason to take a chance on me. Jan 8, 2018, was my first day on set with the OWN hit show "The Have or The Have Nots." I wanted to do costumes and be in wardrobe department. I've now served in the Props department or as a Props Master for six years now." ~ Sean Davis

Props Sean has worked with include:

- A paper plane - We had an invisible string attached to a paper plane and zip lined it through a window from outside.
- 300 Cocaine Bricks – *"Black Mafia Family"* (HULU)
- Different weapons of choice for the villains on *"Ironheart"* (MARVEL)

71

PUBLICIST

Publicists create the 'buzz' that surrounds the release of a film. They get the critics talking.

They are responsible for getting media coverage of the film through having good relationships with journalists and critics. They create press packets, which usually include the film's synopsis, production notes, cast and crew credits and biographies, stills and the electronic press kit (EPK). Film publicists also schedule press screenings for bigger budget movies. Unit publicists invite journalists to the set during shooting.

They handle all major aspects of press relations and keep the distributor and producer informed of PR developments. They look over all publicity materials with consideration of any legal, ethical, and cultural issues. If there's any controversy at any stage, it's the publicist who deals with damage control – and they need to be available at any time of the day and night to do so.

Skills of a Professional Publicist:

- Understanding the Media: Have good contacts in the film and media industries, know the needs of journalists in print, TV, radio and online
- Writing: Write the promotional story of the film, create press packs, devise release plans
- Knowledge of the Film Market: Identify the core audience for a film, know how to reach them and excite them, be aware of box office figures, viewing figures and the film trends
- Flexibility: Thrive in changing situations, enjoy spontaneity
- Persuasion: Network with the influencers in the film industry, such as press, critics and programmers, and pitch and convince them of the strength of the film-

Professional Publicist to Know: **Syreta Oglesby** *(SJO Public Relations)* and Meredith O'Sullivan *(Will Smith)*

72

Rigger

Riggers create digital skeletons for 3D computer-generated (CG) characters. These skeletons, or rigs, are like puppets that define the movements of a character or creature, such as how a big cat runs or how a person's face and mouth move when they sing or how someone raises an eyebrow. They are used by animators as the basis for the movements of their characters.

Riggers start with 3D models in a static pose, created by the modellers. They then create the network of movements for that character. For a singing character, they create rigs for the mouth, tongue, eyes, ears, arms and belly, as well as one for how these parts move together. Animators test rigs and then give feedback to riggers who complete any requested fixes or improvements. The process will continue until both the riggers and the animators are happy with the rigged models (the 3D puppets).

Riggers usually work with characters, but they can also create rigs for anything that moves in an animation.

Skills of a good rigger:

1. Knowledgeable of animation and art
2. Knowledgeable of 3D animation programs
3. Coding: use programming languages, like Python, to automate the rigging process where possible
4. Works well with the other members of the 3D animation pipeline, especially the modellers and animators

73

RIGGING GRIP

A Rigging Grip is a technician who sets up rigging equipment for cameras and lighting before the camera crew arrives on a film or television set. They attach grip and lighting hardware to structures to light the set and support the camera, ensuring the equipment is set up safely and correctly for the director's desired shot. Grips may also be responsible for keeping equipment organized and sometimes performing maintenance. Grips work under the direction of the best boy electric, who reports to the key grip. They may also assist the cinematographer with camera movement to ensure smooth and controlled shots. Grips may need to install lights and complicated rigs in unusual places, and may also be involved in moving camera equipment, such as dollies, cranes, and track.

74

ROTO ARTIST AKA JUNIO VISUAL EFFECTS (VFX) ARTIST

Roto Artists manually draw around and cut out objects from movie frames so that the required parts of the image can be used, a process known as *rotoscoping*. The parts of an image that are wanted after cutting out are known as *mattes*. Roto artists work on the areas of live action frames where computer-generated (CG) images or other live-action images will overlap or interact with the live image. If the live-action camera is not moving within a shot, rotoscoping might involve only one frame. If the camera's moving, roto artists trace the relevant areas of every frame within the shot so that CG can be combined accurately with the live action. Roto artists need to have a keen eye and patience to complete this meticulous and repetitive work. In addition to rotoscoping, roto artists assist in the preparation of material for compositing.

75

RUNNER

Runners are all-purpose helpers in any production studio. They support any and all members in the studio and make sure that everyone has what they need. Runners do a variety of jobs. They deliver materials and messages between departments. They organize meetings and schedules. They keep the office clean and tidy and might work on reception or be responsible for locking up. They also make a lot of tea and coffee, lol. They do whatever professional task needs doing.

A runner is an entry level position. In some studios, runners are seen as the entry point into production management. Some companies might assign runners a mentor and give them training tasks. The runner role can be a good route into the industry for someone without relevant degree education but with a good portfolio and lots of enthusiasm.

76

SCREENWRITER/SCRIPT WRITER

A Screenwriter can write scripts for a variety of mediums (feature films, TV shows, commercials, video games, etc.). They're the ones who create the story, characters, and dialogue.

Professional Script/Screenwriter to Know: **Lekethia Dalcoe** (*"Silo"* on Apple+)

77

SCRIPT EDITOR

Script Editors liaise between the writer of a drama and the TV production company, commissioner, or development producer to ensure that the script is as good as possible.

They might come on board at any point in the script writing process. Sometimes script editors start before the writer. The executive or development producer might want a new drama for 18 to 25-year-olds, set in a nightclub, for example. The script editor might be asked to research ideas or come up with concepts for episodes.

Meanwhile the development producer or editorial head, identifies the right writer for the job. Once the writer is in place, the script editor's role is to support the writer and get the script ready for production. They need to understand how the writer works and appreciate the writer's voice. They might help the writer to develop a storyline or introduce a new character. They are the ones that need to have tactful and creative conversations about budget. They might need to explain there isn't enough money for quite that number of buildings to be blown up, for example.

Typically, there will be several people with comments to make on a script, such as the commissioner, the producer, or the director. The script editor gathers these notes and takes them to the writer in a respectful and considerate way. They also ensure there's continuity between scenes and between episodes and that the script is running to time.

78

SCRIPT SUPERVISOR

Film and TV dramas are usually shot entirely out of sequence. Shooting is organized according to the practicalities of location and availability of cast rather than the unfolding of the story. It's the job of the script supervisor to check each filmed scene can be edited so it will make sense in the end.

During pre-production script supervisors prepare a continuity breakdown: a document which analyses the script in terms of cast, actions, wardrobe and props in scenes and story days. Then they time the script, which is quite a skill. Once filming starts, they closely monitor what's happening to check no dialogue is overlooked and the actions and eye-lines of the actor's match. They keep detailed written and photographic records of dialogue, action, costumes, and props. All camera and lens details are noted along with the slate and scene number information. They keep a progress report of each day's filming which goes to production and the visual effects (VFX) supervisor in the case of VFX shots. These records are invaluable. They mean directors and editors can find what's been shot and what the options are for each scene. They mean that when different takes are edited together, the film is consistent and makes sense.

<u>Skills of Script Supervisor</u>
1. Analysis: Break down, time and itemize scenes in terms of set, costumes, make-up, props and dialogue according to where they are in the story
2. Filmmaking: Understand the art of storytelling through a lens, know what this means in terms of required shots and crossing the line
3. Observation: Have an eagle eye and good memory, have the stamina to remain observant during long filming days
4. Attention to Detail: Be meticulous and methodical in taking precise notes quickly and efficiently
5. Communication: Let the director, actors, crew, hair, make-up and production know about continuity issues

Professional Script Supervisor to Know: **Claire Tanner** ("The Game")

79

SET DESIGNER

Set Designers, or scenic designers, are responsible for the worlds that characters on the stage and screen inhabit. From the rooms to the buildings and outdoor spaces, Set Designers move through to the pieces of furniture that fill them, and even aspects of presentation like the set's angle.

Professional Set Designer to Know: **Rick Carter** *("Back to the Future Part II," + "Jurassic Park")*

80

SET DRESSER

A Set Dresser in film is responsible for selecting, arranging, and setting up objects and elements to create a scene's background and atmosphere. Their work can include placing furniture, hanging pictures, and putting out decorative items like drapery, lighting fixtures, and artwork. Set dressers work under the direction of a production designer and set decorator, and typically have a leadman or lead person as their immediate supervisor. Set dressers' work is important for establishing a film's mood, setting, and time period, and can help make the location of each scene look convincing. Set Dressers can help create a sense of belief in what the audience is seeing, which can help the production stick with viewers long after it's finished.

81

SET MEDIC AND CONSTRUCTION MEDIC

A Set Medic, also known as an EMT or paramedic, is a medical professional who provides emergency assistance to people working on film or TV productions. They are responsible for being on standby to treat injuries or illnesses that may occur to cast or crew members during shooting. Set medics may also advise the production team on safety and medical issues, such as the medical accuracy of a scene. To become a set medic, you typically need to meet the following requirements:

- Be a registered paramedic, EMT, nurse, PA, or doctor
- Have current CPR and EMT certifications
- Have relevant experience, such as at least five years in a 911-type facility
- Have background checks, such as a state and federal CORI database search
- Be comfortable working long hours, sometimes late, and in extreme weather conditions

82

Scientific Consultant

A Scientific Consultant is someone who advises and provides consultation services on scientific matters. In sci-fi movies and other movies/shows that involve scientific concepts, a scientific consultant is usually used. Although many have stated that scientific consultants in entertainment have been doing the work pro bono, there are lucrative career opportunities available as a Hollywood scientific consultant.

83

SHOWRUNNER

A Showrunner is the top-level executive producer of a television series, who outranks other creative and management personnel, including episode directors, in contrast to feature films, in which the director has creative control over the production, and the executive producer's role is limited to investing.

<u>Professional Showrunners to Know</u>

- **Shonda Rhimes** *("Grey's Anatomy")*
- **Lee Daniels** *("Empire")*
- **Quinta Brunson** *("Abbott Elementary")*
- **Issa Rae** *("Insecure")*
- **Donald Glover** *("Atlanta")*
- **Lena Waithe** *("The Chi")*

- **Janine Sherman Barrois** *("Claws")*
- **Quinta Brunson** *("Abbott Elementary")*

84

Software Developer

Software Developers produce the technology required for a visual effects (VFX) project. They create the systems which technical directors (TDs) can use and modify to suit the specific needs of their VFX artists. They also design new digital tools and make sure they fit into existing software systems. This enables the efficient passing of assets from one VFX process to the next. This is a research and development role, which means that it involves working out ways to improve how well digital processes works. Software developers must stay informed about software and technology relevant to their field and beyond. They find innovate ways to enable the artists within the pipeline to complete their work as fast and as well as possible.

85

SOFTWARE ENGINEER

Software Engineers design, develop, look after and test computer software used in broadcasting. They work on a huge variety of projects. For example, they might make sure that a production house's edit suites can access only the footage they have permission to use or might create a system to make sure every piece of music used in a film is logged automatically so that composers are paid quickly.

Software engineers write code that is safe from cyber threats. Senior engineers also know how to write code that could be used on future, bigger versions of the computer system. They get rid of bugs and add fixes for when the code runs into problems or create new features so that the software is more powerful. Whenever a new feature is added to the software, software engineers must write testing plans that explain how to test the software for the engineers using it.

Updated software is added to broadcasting computer systems 24 hours a day, so the new software must be reliable, easy to test and ready to go so that broadcasting isn't disrupted.

Good software engineers are in short supply, so this is a well-paid job where you can work your way up from a trainee to a senior software engineer and principal software engineer.

86

SOUND MIXER

Sound Mixers head up the department responsible for all the sound recorded during filming. This is predominantly dialogue but can include sound effects and atmosphere. Before shooting starts, they meet with the producer and director to discuss the best method of capturing sound alongside the director's shooting style. They visit locations to check for potential sound problems, like passing trains or road noise.

During filming, sound mixers ensure audio from radio and boom microphones is recorded at a good level for every take. If they flag a problem, the director decides whether to do another take or correct it in post-production. Much of sound on a film or TV drama is added in the edit. Speech is often corrected through ADR or automated dialogue replacement: a way of re-recording in a studio. Some of the film sets can be challenging for mixers. Some issues that may arise are costumes rustling, humming from generators and cameras pointed in places where a microphone needs to be.

87

STAKEBED DRIVER

A Stakebed Driver is an essential member of the Production Support department in filmmaking. This position involves operating a stakebed truck to transport equipment, props, and crew members to various locations during film production. The primary role of a Stakebed Driver is to ensure the safe and timely transportation of equipment and personnel to and from filming locations. This includes loading and unloading equipment, securing items for transport, and following strict safety protocols while driving. Stakebed Drivers also play a crucial role in assisting with the logistics of the production, helping to maintain the efficiency of the filmmaking process.

<u>Skills of a Stakebed Driver</u>

- Possess excellent driving skills and be comfortable operating large vehicles
- Attention to detail and the ability to follow directions
- Strong Communication Skills are also beneficial, as Stakebed Drivers may need to coordinate with other crew members to ensure smooth transportation logistics
- Physical strength and stamina are advantageous, as the role may involve heavy lifting and long hours behind the wheel.

88

STEADICAM OPERATOR

As the Steadicam Operator on a film production, you are first and foremost a camera operator responsible for capturing the movements of actors and scenes on film. This role ensures that shots are in focus and that the equipment is set up and working correctly. You take instruction from the director and director of photography, also known as the DOP, DP, or cinematographer, to plan and film specific shots, and work with camera teams, producers, and production managers. This role differs from other camera operator roles in that the motion picture camera is physically connected to your body by a special harness and a pivoted support called a gimbal. The harness allows freedom of movement over uneven surfaces, while the gimbal allows the camera to move smoothly around an axis, creating overall stability for a smooth shot.

Because Steadicam equipment is over eighty pounds and sometimes operated while moving quickly or even running, good physical fitness and strength are required for the role.

89

STOP-MOTION ANIMATORS

Stop-Motion Animators work with puppets or models made from clay or other materials. They move the models of characters by tiny amounts, one frame at a time, so they can be photographed and recorded, as though moving continuously in a sequence. On a large-scale project, such as a feature film, stop-motion animators can be hired for particular skills. For example, some animators might be especially good at working with action, while others excel with charm, comedy or dialogue. Some might also excel in animating certain characters in non-creature objects. Common materials for stop-motion animation include clay or plasticine, paper, or action figures like Lego.

Tools and/or Software Used in Stop Motion

- 3D Printing
- Molding
- Biomedical Field - 3D printers, print body parts, cat scan of a patient with a tumor or in need of operation and create mock operations
- Maya, solid works or Inventor (Software)

Professional Stop Motion Animator to Know: **Brian McClean** @ Laika (*Director of Rapid Prototype*)

Examples of Productions/Films/TV Shows that use Stop Motion

1. *"Coraline"*
2. *"Shaun the Sheep"*
3. *"Postman Pat"*
4. *"Isle of Dogs"*

For more information on Stop Motion Animation, visit https://www.laika.com/

90

STORY EDITOR

A Story Editor in film production is a writer and producer who manages the screenwriting process for movies and television shows. They have many responsibilities, including:

- Developing stories
- Working closely with writers on each draft of their story and script, providing feedback, and suggesting improvements
- Ensuring scripts are suitable for production
- Making sure scripts adhere to practical issues like continuity and correct running time
- Managing the story department
- Assigning story analysts to read scripts, and acting as a liaison between the creative executive staff and the story department
- Overseeing the screenwriting process
- Suggesting new ideas, editing drafts, and approving rewrites
- Collaborating with others
- Working directly with editors, and collaborating with executive producers and showrunners

Story editors may also be involved in producing or editing source footage during pre to postproduction, and writing host dialogue, VO, and dialogue and action pickups.

91

STUNT COORDINATOR

A Stunt Coordinator is a professional who plans and manages stunts for film, television, or live performances. They are usually experienced stunt performers themselves and work closely with the director to achieve the production's vision safely and realistically.

A stunt Coordinator's responsibilities include:

- Casting: Selecting stunt performers
- Planning: Designing and preparing stunt sequences and actions
- Safety: Ensuring the safety of the crew and staff during stunts
- Collaboration: Working with the director, first AD, and stunt performers to create and manage stunts

Professional Stunt Coordinator to Know: **La Faye Baker** - the 1st African American stuntwoman to coordinate a big budget project on HBO *"The Dorothy Dandridge"* story starring Halle Berry. Baker's work has also been seen on Netflix shows and *"Insecure."*

92

SUBTITLER

Subtitlers make it possible for films to be enjoyed by audiences all over the world and by the deaf and hard of hearing. They translate all the dialogue, music and sound effects of a film into two-line written captions that appear on the screen, either in the language in which the film is made or in a foreign language. After carefully watching and listening to the whole film, they write captions with accurate time codes that describe music and sound effects as well as the dialogue and voice-overs. The captions are often punctuated and spelt correctly and should be on the screen long enough to be read easily. Translating subtitlers translate the dialogue and write subtitles in the language for a particular audience.

Once they've done that and checked that all spelling is correct and that captions don't obscure characters' faces, the files are sent to the mastering house (transferring the final soundtrack onto the film in all the various formats). It can then be distributed to cinemas offering subtitled screenings or to cinemas around the world.

93

Supervising Sound Editor

Supervising Sound Editors manage the team that looks after each part of the sound of a film or TV project. This includes those responsible for dialogue, additional dialogue recording (ADR), sound effects, background sounds and Foley. Their role varies according to the budget of the production. On lower budget projects they start work when the picture editor has achieved picture lock – the point at which the director or executive producer has given the final approval for the picture edit. On bigger budget projects, they start work before shooting begins and appoint specialist sound editors to supervise separate teams for each area of work. After picture lock, supervising sound editors attend a "spotting session" with the director and other sound editors. They discuss any concepts for the overall feel of the sound (naturalistic or stylized), check every sound effect and line of dialogue to see what's needed. They will then have a hands-on role in creating the overall soundtrack for every discipline.

Supervising Sound Editors are responsible for the sound budget and for organizing the workflow. From sound editorial, Foley recording, ADR sessions, pre-mix to final mix, they make plans for any special requirements. After the final mix, supervising sound editors usually oversee the creation of the different deliverables, including a music and effects version which allows dialogue to be replaced with dialogue in different languages.

94

Texture Artist aka Texture Painter, Texturing Artist, Visual Effects Artist (VFX), 3D Modelling & Texture Artist

Texture Artists make surfaces look realistic on computer-generated (CG) 3D models. They rough objects up or they make them shine *(i.e. Scales on a crocodile's skin, reflections on car doors, skid marks on roads, creases in trouser)*

They start with a 3D model created by a modelling artist that is usually a plain grey shape. The texture artists paint the details onto the surface of the models until they look like a photograph.

Texture artists sometimes create textures from scratch, so they have a good understanding of different kinds of real-world materials. Sometimes they work from a library of stock textures, or they might use photographs.

Once a texture artist is happy with the textured surface that they have created, they can 'bake' (copy using a VFX program's 'baking tool') the texture from one surface so that it can be used elsewhere as well.

Tools used by Texture Artists

- Graphics Software
    - Adobe After Effects
    - Dreamweaver
    - Illustrator
    - Photoshop

- 3D modelling, Sculpting and Painting Software
Blender
    - 3ds Max
    - Maya
    - Mudbox
    - ZBrush
    - Substance Painter
    - Substance Designer
    - Quixel

95

TRANSPORTATION CAPTAIN AND/OR TRANSPORTATION COORDINATOR

In this profession, you are responsible for getting people and equipment to set. They organize a plan and budget for conveying where everyone and everything needs to be. The driver takes talent, crew, and equipment to and from the studio or location.

96

VIRTUAL PRODUCTION (VP)

Virtual Production (VP) is a filmmaking technique that combines physical and virtual elements to create realistic environments and effects on a virtual set. Virtual Production helps filmmakers, before the script process, creative VR virtual cameras to solve creative problems. Virtual production enables filmmakers to visualize various aspects of their film before, during, and after production, for both live-action elements and visual effects or animated content. It uses technologies like computer-generated imagery (CGI), augmented reality (AR), motion capture, and real-time 3D engines to create photorealistic sets that are displayed on large LED walls behind physical sets. Cameras are synced with the game engines to enhance realism and depth of perspective. VP can be used in pre- and post-production and is more efficient and artist-friendly than traditional workflows. It allows creators to visualize and experiment with scenes much earlier, which can inspire more ambitious storytelling. It also eliminates the need for multiple post-production revisions and allows for more accurate and immediate feedback.

To do VP, you'll need at least a camera, virtual reality equipment, LED walls or green screen materials, a computer, software, and other resources and tools. The computer should have a fast processor and a high-performance graphics card to run the software and tools. A virtual reality headset, such as the Oculus Quest or HTC Vive, is also essential for previewing and manipulating virtual environments in real-time.

James Cameron's *Avatar* in 2009 was the first film to officially use VP.

Other films that have used VP include:

- *Oblivion* (2013)
- *The Jungle Book* (2016)
- *Rogue One: A Star Wars Story*

97

Visual Effects (VFX) Supervisor

A Visual Effects (VFX) Supervisor is a key role in film production, responsible for overseeing the creation and integration of visual effects into a production. They work on a project from the beginning of preproduction and are the main point of contact between the VFX studio and the film's director or producer. VFX supervisors need to have a combination of artistic, managerial, listening, and communication skills, as well as several years of experience and the skills of an outstanding VFX artist.

They often have a degree in Computer Science, Animation, or Visual Effects, and proven senior-level management experience is important.

Professional VFX Supervisor to Know: **Greg Anderson** (*"Luke Cage"* + *"Spiderman"*)

98

VOCAL CONTRACTOR

A Vocal Contractor is required for vocal groups of 3 or more singers. Any SAG-AFTRA singer can act as a vocal contractor. He/she is responsible for handling the paperwork required and choosing singers based on the musical style and skills required by the project.

Professional Vocal Contractor to Know: **Carmen** (*"The Neighborhood"*)

99

VIDEO PLAYBACK OPERATOR AKA VIDEO ASSIST OPERATOR (VAO) OR VIDEO TAPE OPERATOR (VTR)

A Video Playback Operator is a vital member of the film production team. They are responsible for capturing and displaying images from film or digital cameras on video monitors for the director and crew to view in real time and play back immediately. This allows the director to confirm elements like camera focus, framing, and choreography for accuracy. The playback is also recorded for continuity checks and to create a complete archive of the shots taken.

VAOs work closely with other departments, including the director, script supervisor, camera teams, and VFX crews. They often manage a team of assistants and trainees on larger shoots. VAOs must also ensure that all footage is stored carefully on hard disc or digital media, and that their equipment is packed and ready for use the next day.

<u>Skills of a Good VAO</u>

- Concentration: Be alert and ready to respond immediately
- Video Knowledge: Understand video playback equipment, cables, wireless links, and signals and formats
- Film Production Knowledge: Understand film cameras and lighting, and the roles of other crew members
- Communication: Be able to work as part of a team and liaise with other departments
- Problem-Solver: Be able to diagnose and correct faults

100

WALKIE PA

The Walkie PA is the right hand to the Key PA. They are responsible for all walkies a production uses. The Walkie PA trouble shoots walkie issues and communicates for the Director and Director of Photography to the Assistant Director team. They also fill in for the Key PA when needed.

101 BONUS

WRITER'S ASSISTANT

Writer's Assistants are people that assist writers of television shows, movies and other media projects while creating scripts. Often, writers can focus on the larger concepts, dialogue, and descriptions for a show while the writer's assistant might organize their notes or take additional notes for review. They might provide additional administrative support to writers.

Duties of a Writer's Assistant

- Proofreading scripts, pitches, and covers for stories
- Fact-checking writers' works
- Researching for new concepts
- Scheduling assignments for writers
- Inputting and managing data
- Answering calls and managing email boxes

Mastery of Skills

*Place an **X** next to each skill that describes you! Circle each skill that you desire to master and each day, dedicate time to master that skill.*

Great Eye for Detail ______

Strong Leadership ______

Strong Communication ______

Interpersonal Skills ______

Know Different Languages ______

Desire to Travel ______

Construction ______

Carpentry ______

Good Physical Condition ______

Find Solutions to Problems ______

Work within Budgets ______

Keep books (Accounting) ______

Good at Math ______

Good with Finances ______

Good eye for the aesthetic and form ______

Punctual ______

Music Producer ______

Great with Customer Service ______

Strong Work Ethic ______

Good at Design, Architecture ______

Knowledgeable of Animation ______

Run Errands – Have a Valid Driver's License ______

Enthusiastic ______

Listen to and Follow Directions Precisely ______

Good at Managing paperwork ______

Understands Anatomy, Physics – How things Move ______

Good at Negotiation ______

Good at Finances & Budgets ______

Discretion ______

Works Well Under Pressure ______

Works Within a Timeline ______

Organized ______

Coding ______

Understands Contracts ______

Interpersonal Skills ______

Art: Be able to draw ______

Good at Collaboration ______

Team Player ______

Maintaining Logs (Timesheets) ____

Good at Math ______

Good at Science ______

Singer ____

Musician ____

Sound Engineer ______

Think Quickly ______

Flexible ______

Resourceful ______

Own a Reliable Vehicle ______

Thinks Quickly ______

Attentive to Detail ______

Punctual ______

Scheduling (Meetings, Travel)

SOFTWARE AND TOOLS TO CONSIDER LEARNING

How well do you know or have utilized any of the software below? Place an X next to each software/application that you own. Circle each software that you desire to master. Homework: Each day, dedicate time to master that skill.

Microsoft Office _______

Excel _______

Photoshop _______

Google Docs _______

Google Sheets _______

Canva _______

Adobe Photoshop _______

Coding

Python _______

C++ _______

Compositing, Digital Painting, 3D modelling, Sculpting and Painting Software

3ds Max _______

After Effects _______

Arnold _______

V-Ray _______

Blackmagic Fusion _______

Houdini _______

Maya _______

Mental Ray _______

Nuke _______

Substance 3D Designer _______

RenderMan _______

Blender _______

3ds Max _______

Maya _______

Mudbox _______

ZBrush _______

Substance Painter _______

Quixel _______

Graphics Software

Adobe After Effects _______

Dreamweaver _______

Illustrator _______

Websites to Assist in Pursuing Your Passion in the Arts

Careers in Film and Television - www.ScreenSkills.com

Stunt Coordinator - https://lafayebaker.com/

Script Supervisor - https://www.youtube.com/watch?v=r6aiuLBp1Jc

Visual Effects - www.scanlinevfx.com

Drawing and Illustration Tools - www.hotdoor.com

Electrician License + Certification - https://www.electricianschooledu.org/state-by-state-licensing-guide/

IATSE LOCAL - https://www.iatselocal52.org/

Backstage West - https://www.backstage.com/

Stop Motion Animation - https://www.laika.com/

ABOUT THE AUTHOR

Ashley Támar, known as the muse & protégé of Prince, gained notoriety for co-writing their Grammy-nominated duet "Beautiful, Loved, and Blessed." A Hollywood Music in Media Award Recipient (HMMA) for Best New Song in New Media (2022), Ms. Davis is currently on tour with the Stewart Copeland Orchestra and a featured soloist on the "Police Deranged for Orchestra" album. Adding to her jaw-dropping career, Ashley's versatility translates to behind-the-scenes as well as a Music Supervisor, Clearance, and Licensing Coordinator for various television/film projects: "Ladies First: The Women in Hip Hop" (NETFLIX)," "Trap Jazz" (HULU), "Three Ways" (HULU), "Cherish the Day," (Season II/OWN), "That Damn Michael Che," (HBO MAX) and more.

Ashley has graced the Walt Disney Hall stage with the LA Philharmonic, guest starred in both "Chippendales" (HULU) and "BRUH" (BET+), receiving raved reviews in Broadway classics: "Ain't Misbehavin," "Motown the Musical," and "A Night with Janis Joplin" where she was nominated as Best Featured Actress. Ms. Davis is an alum of University of Southern California's Thornton School of Music and the author of an edutainment book and workbook: "100 Things to Know as an Independent Music Artist." With four independent albums released independently, Ashley displayed jaw-dropping performances on NBC's "The Voice: Season X" and is internationally recognized for her tear-jerking ballads and acting in numerous Tyler Perry/LionsGate productions.

Though music is a conduit for reaching people through song, Ashley Támar has successfully initiated various community outreach projects: The Syren Arts Academy, the College, Career, and Empowerment Summit, the Támar Talks Podcast and DocFest. Ashley has performed an 11-city national tour "Támar featuring Prince" as well as on Good Morning America, Saturday Night Live, the NAACP Image Awards, the BRIT Awards and has been featured in numerous magazines such as Glamour, Billboard, PEOPLE, and VIBE.

For Booking Information, please contact us below!
info@syrenmusicgroup.com
www.AshleyTamar.com

www.ingramcontent.com/pod-product-compliance
Lightning Source LLC
Chambersburg PA
CBHW072047150726
47996CB00015B/2005